Unnecessary Suffering

by

Derbin Liles

authorHOUSE

1663 LIBERTY DRIVE, SUITE 200
BLOOMINGTON, INDIANA 47403
(800) 839-8640
www.authorhouse.com

First published by AuthorHouse 06/21/04

ISBN: 1-4184-2142-1 (e)
ISBN: 1-4184-2141-3 (sc)

Printed in the United States of America
Bloomington, Indiana

This book is printed on acid-free paper.

Bible verses from King James Version Bible

Table of Contents

Book Dedication

First and foremost, I would like to thank God. I thank Him for saving my soul and for sparing my life through bad situations. As you read this book, there are times when I'm not supposed to be here; but thank you, Jesus.

Second, I would like to thank my mother, Ella, for raising three children on her own and doing a wonderful job. While growing up, we thought we just weren't allowed to do anything wrong. There was always punishment following our wrong doing. I remember when you would punish me, Sinatra and Patrick. You would always say I'm doing this because I love you and I want you to know right from wrong. I would think, this ain't love. If you love me like you say you do, forget about what I just did.

In the end, everything paid off. We grew up to be independent, young women and an independent young man. We made you a grandmother of seven. We know you love each and every one of them. Even though we are miles apart, I love you more today than I did yesterday. Thank you, Mom for disciplining us when there was a need. Love you, your daughter, Derbin W. Liles.

Special Thanks

Thank you Mrs. Patricia Taylor for being such a great typist.

Thank you Mrs. Sara Overby for making sure the I's were dotted and the T's were crossed.

God bless you both!

Introduction

Writing this book was laid on my heart by God himself. At first I didn't want to write it because it would expose me and my trials. God said to me, many women go through the same thing you went through. Some go through worse. If one woman reads this story, that will be one woman who listened. He wanted me to write this to spread the Goodness and to help suffering women to know that the answer doesn't lie in these worldly things, nor does it lie in our limited thinking, but it lies solely in Him. Turn to the Lord. His knowledge and understanding surpasses all understanding.

Early Childhood - Growing Up Poor

I was born July 15, 1967, to a young woman named Ella Mae. I, Derbin Liles, am the middle child an older sister Sinatra and younger brother Patrick. We grew up poor not knowing what we were going to eat some nights. My mother who was an assistant teacher found it very hard to raise three children and keep us fed and clothed. My Mom decided to go back to school while we were small children. We were left with different babysitters until she found out the young lady she let keep us would let her children hit us and scratch us. We weren't allowed to hit back because she would beat us if we hit her children. After my Mom took us away from the babysitters, my sister Sinatra became the sitter, which caused her to grow up faster than she anticipated growing up.

I remember when my sister would fix my hair every night and put some old panties on my head and send me to bed. Of course there were times she had to beat my brother to make him go to bed because he thought he was the man of the house and he could stay up as late as he wanted to. We all slept in one bedroom because the house was so small, there wasn't enough room for us each to have our own room. We had our own beds, though. There was a bunk bed and one single bed, one closet, and one dresser. Boy, was that room small.

Our kitchen was small as well. The floor had a big hole in it and when Mom would cook something we didn't like, when she turned her head, one by one we would run to the hole up under the sink and pour the food out to the chickens and the dogs that slept near that hole. Then Mom would come in the kitchen to put her plate in the sink, She would see all of our plates empty and she would say, "here, eat the rest of this so I won't have to throw this food away because I hate wasting food." As she emptied the food on our plates, we looked at each other in disgust. Mom would also wash clothes every other Saturday. I guess she got paid bi-weekly so we went to the laundrymat when she could afford to wash. We had to walk about three blocks to the laundrymat. We didn't have a car. Sometimes I cried on the inside, not letting anyone know I was hurting, because I wanted us to have things that other people had. Sometimes, Mom would fill the baskets up so full that our hands became scarred while we were walking. The kids would talk about us, but my sister told me that I had to learn how to ignore ignorant people because people talk about you whether you do good or bad. My brother and I were the fighters but my sister was the one who kept calm. We didn't play like other children did, because my Mom kept us busy to keep us out of trouble. We went to church every Sunday and would stay there all day long.

What got me is if we saw something we liked and told my Mom about it, she would say, "Describe it to me again." My sister and I would go on describing how the outfit was made and Mom would say, Go look in my closet and see how much material I have." My sister and I would look at each other and get sad, because instead of Mom going out to buy us the outfit, she would make us walk down to the clothing store, Royal's, and get her simplicity #264. She would make us that outfit we described. Oh yes, she made clothes too. My Mom was single and she had to learn how to save money. She was also a barber. She cut my brother's hair also. My sister and I would get pampered every now and again when Mom could afford it. She would send us to the beautician to get our hair straightened. Of course, no one wanted to mess with my hair because they said it was too long and they had things to do on Saturday, and they didn't want to spend all day on my head.

My brother and I were very athletic. When we did go outside to play, as we took a break from studying, children from different neighborhoods would ask my brother and me if we wanted to race against their street and whoever would lose would have to give up $3.00. Of course, I told my brother we had to win because we didn't have $3.00 and we knew Mom wasn't going to give it to us. Three dollars would buy us a whole lot of penny cookies and candy. Of course, we had to find two more people to run with us, because we were running a relay race from one street to the next. We used a stick for the baton. My brother ran the first leg and I ran the last leg. We put the two slow people in the middle, and of course, we won every time. That $3.00 sure did come in handy, because I gave my brother $1.50. We would go to Bobby's Grocery Store on the corner from our house and buy 100 cookies and 50 pieces of candy each. My sister would ask for some of our goodies. We eventually shared with her. She didn't work as hard as we did to eat candy and cookies.

Trips to North Carolina

Every summer, the day after school was out, Mom would pack our clothes and Middlesex, North Carolina, is where we would reside for the two months, from the end of June to August 15 with our maternal grandmother, Mozelle Silver.

Living in the country was not my thing. I hated going to North Carolina because there was no bathroom, no running water, no nearby stores - nothing but a path full of family that told my grandmother everything we did. My grandmother had 14 children. My mother is the seventh child. Sometimes I wondered why we had to stay in the woods because Grandma made us work in the cucumber field and around the house, which was no summer vacation to me.

I loved my grandmother very much. She would load us up in the station wagon and take us riding around town and to Raleigh to visit my Aunt Mary who is my mother's second oldest sister. On the way back to Middlesex, Grandma would stop at the bakery and get us a lot of snacks and goodies and when we got on the family path, and halfway to her house,

Grandma would speed down that bumpy path just to see her Grandbabies smile and, boy, did we smile.

My aunts and uncles think I favor my Grandma so much. I really miss her. If she could see how many great-grandchildren she has now, she would say, "Come and get the chil'ren. I can't feed all of them." At the same time, she will have jars and jars of preserves and a freezer full of food.

One summer morning on a Saturday, Grandma was cooking breakfast while a few cousins were outside playing with the pigs and chickens, riding bicycles and spending time trying to figure out how much land Grandma had by getting lost to find their way home. Of course, I was the one that was in the house because it was too hot to go outside. I remember everyone, except for my Grandmother, walking into another room to look at something that was on television. I stayed behind to watch and smell the food. All of a sudden, this cord fell down in front of me from the ceiling. Naturally being a child and curious as well I stood on a ladder and picked up the live wire and tried to put it back together. My Grandma just happened to turn around to see what I was doing and before I knew it, I was on the floor. Grandma pushed me off the ladder onto the floor and said, "No, you can't touch that. You are going to kill yourself." I remember looking at her as if she was crazy.

Every Sunday morning Grandma took us to church in Spring Hope, North Carolina. She had a lot of relatives there and that was also where she attended Clifton Chapel Baptist Church. My sister and I used to sing a lot, so every Sunday we would have to do a selection before the preacher would preach. I used to love to sing. Singing was one of my favorite things to do, if I wasn't cheering, running track, or hanging out with friends.

I was so glad when August 15th would come because I knew it was time for us to go back home. I loved my family, but it was nothing like sleeping in my own bed -- even if it was the bottom of a bunk. We went to North Carolina every summer until I turned thirteen years old.

Beginning Stages of Adulthood

After I became a teenager, I began to "smell" myself. "Smelling" yourself is an expression used by "old folks" that means you are trying to do things that you are not old enough nor mature enough to do. I was dating an older boy whom my mother knew nothing about because she was still in college getting her master's degree this time. The only way my Mom found about this boy is that he thought he was in love with me and I thought I was in love with him. He bought me a promise ring. In the late '70's early '80's, when young men thought they were in love, they bought the young ladies promise rings. The promise ring had my name on one side and his name on the other. This was the beginning of me believing that "I had it going on." He was Latino and I believed that he knew how to treat me. Yeah! Of course my Mom found out about the ring and made me give it back. I refused to give the ring back so she took it off my finger and took the ring to the boy's place of employment and forbid him to see me again. I cried for about three weeks - until he started dating someone else and had my name taken off the ring and had the next girl's name put on it. I thought, "What a jerk."

When I was fourteen, we began to see a change in my Mom's lifestyle. She had met a man. He bought her a gray, 4-door, 1978 Granada. Oh yes, we had it going on. When we rode down the street, my sister, my brother and I would hang our arms out the window and of course I had to be seen. I would yell at someone I knew from a distance just so they could see we had a car.

My sister was 16. She had a job at Burger King. She would buy my brother and me school clothes to take some of the pressure off my Mom and, of course, we were so unappreciative. If we couldn't go pick out the clothes we wanted, we didn't want anything. My sister didn't care. She said if I didn't wear what she bought, she would. My sister was also at that state of "smelling" herself. She was into boys and all of a sudden she became high-minded. She was a varsity cheerleader and I was a junior varsity cheerleader. She was captain of the varsity cheerleaders. We were very competitive towards each other because we had to come up with new cheers and new chants for the team. We were also at the age where we wanted to hang out after the football and basketball games. Mom wouldn't let us. She knew what time the games ended, how long it would take us to walk home, and everything.

One particular night after Homecoming, I was crowned Miss Junior Varsity Cheerleader and Sinatra was crowned Miss Varsity Cheerleader. We decided to stay for the after party. About an hour into the party some of my friends were running up to me saying your Mom is here, "Your Mom is here, and she's looking for you and Sinatra!" We found each other out of all of those people in that gymnasium and we ran hand in hand across the bridge through the park up three blocks until we reached the front door. We took off our outfits and jumped in the bed so we could pretend that we had been home for a while. The alibi was we saw her leaving when we were turning the corner to come into the yard.

My sister always came up with brilliant ideas. She also said "Der, if we happen to get a whipping, just remember we had a good time while we were out there." We laughed and waited nervously for that front door to come open. When Mom opened that door, her words were, "Get up. You weren't here when I left. Don't pretend you are asleep. Get up now." My sister said, If we get a whipping, I'll go first." She would also say, "If you squeeze your butt in, it won't hurt as bad." My sister was a soldier. She didn't cry when she walked out of my Mom's room. I told her how many licks she got. She told me, she'll count mine and "Don't forget to squeeze tight." Yeah right! When Mom pulled her arm back, I was calling Jesus. I was always scared of that big black leather belt. I would bruise really easy. After the killing, I would go and show my Mom what she did to my skin. She would say, Oh, go get the belt so I can give you some more."

Mom was very strict on me and my sister. I guess she didn't want to end up a Grandma too soon. When Sinatra turned 17 she felt like she was real grown so she left home to pursue a career as a live-in girlfriend with this Latino fellow she fell in love with. She got pregnant at the tender age of 18. She had my oldest niece, Kocell Dejesus. After Kocell was born, my Mom also changed. She wasn't as strict on me like she was with my sister. I could have company at the age of 15, but couldn't go anywhere but in the front yard and talk. Sinatra would bring Kocell over every weekend and I would just hold her and kiss her because she was more like my little sister than my niece. I believe Kocell changed everybody. Kocell also made me not want any kids of my own.

During my senior year, which was 1984, my Mom decided to move to another county. I cried because she waited until my senior year to move and I wanted to graduate from the high school I had attended for three years, which was majority all-black school. Plus, I had made captain of the Varsity Cheerleading squad. Mom said, "Well the new school you're going to has a good cheering squad. You can cheer for them." During the summer of '84 we moved to Clewiston, Florida, and I hated it because I worked so hard at my previous school to get some things accomplished. I broke up with my then-boyfriend, Simon. A long distance relationship wasn't my thing. When school started in August, I dreaded going because Clewiston High had no pep and the majority of their students were white. When I started attending the school on a regular basis, I knew one young lady there because she had attended Glades Central High during our freshmen year. Her parents moved to Clewiston because they wanted their children in a different environment. This young lady remembered me as soon as she saw me but after a while she began "playa hating." I found out later that she stopped liking me because the most popular guy in school had a crush on me." Boy was he fine! He played football, and ran track. He was very athletic. I met Larry ,in my first period class. He used to sit in front of me with his hands on his chin, saying, "One day you are going to be my girlfriend." I turned around to see who he was talking to. He said, "I'm talking to you." I would say, No you're not, because I'm not interested in nobody at this school." I thought

I could turn him off by telling him I already had a boyfriend. He said he didn't care. I would find myself hiding from this boy. He had a few of his classes changed to mine, even chorus. I finally gave in and told him I would go out with him after two months of him pursuing me.

He would put my name in the newspaper with his. I thought this guy must really like me. When I told him he had to meet my Mom and my stepfather he agreed. I asked my Mom could he come over one Sunday for dinner. She said, "Yes, she would love to meet him. I gave Larry , directions to my house. As soon as he came in the house, "he said my brother lives right behind y'all," and my Mom said, "Oh, Lord." Larry , was not shy.

I was working at Winn Dixie after school and Larry would pick me up from work most of the time. I knew Larry was popular and back then girls did whatever they had to do in order to get him to notice them. Larry and I dated a year before we had intercourse. He was the one I lost my virginity to. I was 17 years old. Larry was talking about marriage, but I didn't want to marry him because he was offered a full football scholarship. I wanted him to pursue his career. We graduated May 30, 1985.

Beginning Stages of Adulthood

One fateful morning after about four years of not going to North Carolina, I told my Mom that I wanted to go and visit my grandmother. I didn't tell Larry that I was leaving because if I had told him, I knew he would have tried to stop me from going. I went to North Carolina around the end of June 1985. My niece Kocell was one year old and my sister was pregnant with my second niece, Latrecia.

When I arrived in North Carolina, I told my Mom that I wanted to stay with my grandma. I didn't want to tell her the real reason for wanting to stay, which was to put Larry behind me . My second niece was born September 1, 1985, and I was in North Carolina thinking I was grown and doing grown folks things. I found my biological father who was remarried with threestep- daughters. We currently have no relationship because he has missed so much time that he can't possibly make it up.   During 1986, my sister had two daughters and was expecting her third child. She had my nephew Edwin, August 28, 1986.

Marriage - Divorce

I met Jim in November 1985. I wasn't interested in him at first but as the months progressed he began to look okay. I thought I would never have children, especially with Jim because he was jealous, didn't like to work, and wanted nothing out of life. On February 24, 1987, we had our first child and named him after Jim. On this day I was so depressed.

I was with a man who was very violent. Jim had a history of abusing women. The biggest mistake any woman or young lady can make is to move in the parent's home along with the person you are dating. He also had two sisters that resided there. I moved to his mother's house in 1986. I chose to learn the hard way, and it was one experience I will never forget.

I didn't know Jim was as violent as he was and his family always took up for his wrong doing. When I first met his youngest sister, she had two children whom she didn't care for. Her oldest was a boy and the youngest was an eight-month-old girl. I had never heard a child talk back to their parents until I met this family. The children would tell their Mom to shut up and she would do just that.

Jim and I slept in the room across from his youngest sister, who thought I was her baby sitter because when I would get up some mornings, her children would be sitting in the living room by themselves watching tv. When I asked where was their mom, the oldest would say she left. Jim was never at home. He would get up in the morning and leave with his friends and I wouldn't see him sometimes for days. There are so many times I wanted to leave but he always talked me out of it.

During the nine months I carried my son, Jim was never home. He never went to my doctor's appointments with me. I would walk to the doctor because I had to go. I was what the doctor called a high-risk patient. My doctor told me that my blood pressure was so high that whatever I was doing, I needed to release it or whomever I was with they were making me sad to the point where the baby was getting depressed. I thought I was in love and I didn't want to seem like I was a failure in my relationship by having to return home to Florida to live with my Mom.

I remember one cold day in November I had been at the doctor's office all day long. Jim sent his oldest sister, whom he had a close relationship with, to pick me up from the doctor's office. She saw me standing outside waiting for someone to pick me up. She pulled up to where I was and said, "Jim said you were going to give me a few dollars for gas." Remember, I'm six months pregnant with no job, no money or anything else. When I told her I didn't have any money and that he lied to her, she pulled off and left me standing at the clinic. Yes, I did curse her out and called her every name in the book. I began to walk because it was almost dark. As I was walking down New Bern Avenue in Raleigh, North Carolina, I began to cry because

I often wondered how any person can be so mean especially to a woman with child. I still wasn't tired because I continued to stay with them.

Around my ninth month, it began to snow and I had washed mine and Jim's clothes and refused to put his clothes up. As I was getting ready to walk out the kitchen door, Jim kicked me in my back and I fell to the ground in the snow. His Mom was very sympathetic - she defended me alot.

I went into labor two days later. Jim came to the hospital. He was a terrible sight to see because he was drunk. I had my son 12 hours later. I went back to their home three days later. When I walked in from the hospital, there was a lot of whispering going on. One of his sisters asked what's the baby's name? I replied I named him after Jim . The only comment I heard was, "oh."

I spoke to my Mom but I never told her what was going on. I knew I was with the wrong man, but then again, I felt like I needed to be there with him. When my Mom would call me from Florida, his youngest sister would pretend as if my Mom dialed the wrong number or she didn't know who I was. There were words passed between her and I, but of course Jim took his sister's side.

During the winter of 1987, Jim came into some money. I told him it was time for us to get our own place. He agreed. Our first apartment was in the projects but it was our place. It seemed like as soon as we moved out, Jim started acting crazier. He would leave for days at a time, especially when he got paid. I was receiving WIC for the baby so getting his milk was not a problem.

Jim stopped paying the bills. The lights were turned off and it was cold. My son and I slept really close together to keep warm. When daylight came, I would see Jim go by the house in his car. I guess he was going to work. In the afternoon around 5:00 PM, I would run to the window and see him ride by while my son and I sat in the cold with no lights and no food.

One day I cried and prayed to the Lord and asked for forgiveness before I did it. My baby had no food, so I put him in his stroller and we walked to the supermarket up the street. I stole a can of Enfamil baby formula and a box of food. I asked the next door neighbors could they feed me and they did without asking any questions. I didn't want anybody to know what I was going through so I came up with a lie about not having any food.

Jim came home when all the money was gone and tried to fight. He got the shock of life because that's when I began to fight back. He saw a different me. I guess I never fought back when I was living with his family because when you live with other people, you have to respect their house. I wouldn't let his family keep my son because they spread rumors saying my son didn't belong to Jim. Of course, he denied what I heard wasn't true even though it came from his aunt.

I finally got the strength to get out and find me a job while my grandma kept my son. I went to work through a temporary service and held that job for almost two years. I met different people from the job who lived near my house so they would offer to drop me off at home.

Independence was headed in my direction. As I began to have an income, the rent was too far gone to try to catch up. We were evicted. I was back to square one at Jim's mother's house. After approximately two weeks, she asked us to leave because she didn't have enough room for three extra people. Jim asked his baby sister if we could move in with her. At the time it was convenient for her because her lights were disconnected. She needed the money to get her lights turned on. I didn't want to move in but there was no other way around it. We stayed about a month before she asked us to leave because she wanted her privacy. I understood. Once again, we had no where to go.

Jim had a car. He decided to the only thing left for us to do is to live in the car. We had all of our clothes in the trunk and the food I bought we kept in the back seat. Jim dropped me off at work early and I would go in the bathroom to wash up and brush my teeth. Then I would sit at my desk as if I just left home. This went on for approximately one month. We finally moved into a rooming house until I was approved for an apartment in my name. We stayed in that one room house for about three months. With Jim still not working my income was what we depended on to get by. After moving into our second apartment, things still had not gotten better, Jim would come home around 2:00 a.m. or later drunk, talking loud and looking for something to eat. I let him know I was not his mother, which started a fight.

Pain and Suffering

There were times I would walk in the wee hours of the morning to my Grandma's house. My grandma used to say when you are tired you will know and so will he. I stayed with Grandma until the anger left. Then I found myself back in the same situation again. Each day with Jim was the same thing, but a different day.

We eventually lost the second apartment, but I was determined I was not going back to live with his Mom. I went and resided with my grandma and my cousin, Cameron, for a few months until the passing of my stepfather, John.

John was the only father I had known for years until I became of age and met my biological father. John departed this earth May 1988. Even though he lived with us and married my mother, he had a deep dark secret. John was a womanizer, an adulterer. One woman was not enough for him. He didn't heed to the warnings God had given him, so he paid for his wrong doings with his life.

After the funeral, I remained in Florida for approximately six months. I was happy being home with my family. I didn't want to go back to North Carolina because I was so unhappy there. I also didn't want my family to know how bad I was suffering. When I got on the train back to North Carolina, I cried most of the 15-hour trip. I didn't understand why I was going back to North Carolina. At the time, it wasn't meant for me to understand.

When I arrived in Raleigh, I didn't call Jim. I called a friend to pick us up from the train station. She couldn't keep a secret because after I arrived at Grandma's house a couple of hours later Jim was at the door. My Grandma was so furious. She told him, If you want her, you need to straighten up and act like a man. Find her a place to stay and keep it." I couldn't get mad because Grandma was so right.

I eventually found another job and another place to live. What I found out about John when I was in Florida made me very cautious (so I thought). But one thing I can say, I was NOT going to tolerate any more nonsense. My backbone was back.

In 1988 I had an office job and stayed there for three years. My son was in home daycare until he turned five years old. In 1990 I found another job working for the government and my sister had her fourth child, Charlie, Jr. Things still weren't good but they were better. I used to say, "I want me a car because I got tired of people picking me up from work when they would think about me." A lot of times, I would be sitting outside of the job, waiting for hours for someone to pick me up.

I remember Jim's sister saying, "how will you get a car with no license?" She didn't know I knew how to drive, but I couldn't find anyone to take me to get my license. I became good friends with one of my coworkers and he put me on his insurance long enough for me to get my driver's license.

My first car was a 1980 Buick Century. It was a good running car for a few years. Then I traded it in and obtained a Dodge Shadow. By this time I was still working for the government and still with Jim. Things had turned around. I was making all of the household decisions.

During 1992, Jim and I sat down and had a talk. I gave him an ultimatum. We had been dating since 1986 and had a son together; therefore, I wanted to know why we couldn't get married or we should go our separate ways. My, what a mistake. We set the wedding date for February 14th - Valentine's Day. Mistake #1: I paid for everything from his wedding band to the preacher and then from the best man's tuxedo to Jim's tuxedo, from the food, alcohol, etc. Jim did absolutely nothing but talk junk.

The wedding was planned to take place at his mother's house. I invited my Mom but she said she didn't want to come because I was making a major mistake. My biological father gave me away. My son was the ring bearer. The wedding took place in his Mom's home. It was small. The presiding pastor could not pronounce my name. The groom was drunk because he had hung out all night at a strip club. The best man was high and I was having second thoughts. Before the ceremony began, Jim came in the back where I was getting dressed and asked me if he could have the keys to my car. I told him no because the wedding was about to start in less than an hour and before I knew it he was calling me stupid. I sat down in a chair and said to myself, "Do you really want to go through with this marriage?"

As I was sitting down getting my thoughts together Jim came back, pushed the door open, and said, "Oh by the way I need to see that engagement ring that's on your finger." I asked him why. He said, because I didn't get you a wedding ring. I asked him why? I had given him the money to buy me a ring - even if it was just a wedding band. By that time tears started rolling down my face because this whole relationship was a complete joke.

I asked him what did he do with the money that I gave him? He replied, he didn't remember. As Jim turned and walked out the door, I remember this inner voice saying, "It's not too late. You're not married yet." As I proceeded to walk out from the back room, I was going out to let everyone know that the wedding was off. I wasn't ready but when I peeped around the corner and saw all those people sitting and smiling and having conversation among each other, I turned around went back to the back of the house and began to cry. I had second thoughts, but then again I had already paid for everything and everybody was in place and waiting on me. I thought that it would go to waste if I didn't go out and meet my so-called groom as we planned. I dried my eyes about ten times before I said I was ready.

My Dad finally came to my rescue to see if I was okay. I could not bring myself to tell him the truth. My brother had come from Georgia and he said to me, "I don't think you want to do this." My Dad said, "No, she's okay. Those are just tears of joy." Boy, if he only knew.

After going through almost an hour of bitterness, I found myself standing at the door arm in arm with my Dad as I made my way down the aisle to render my precious life to someone I lost all respect for.

When the preacher asked me to repeat my vows after him, I did not look at Jim as I was saying my vows. The preacher told me to look at Jim but I couldn't because reality had set in and I was standing at the altar ruining my life.

After Jim said his vows and I said mine, I began to cry again because I was so angry. As I looked at his finger he had on a $400.00 wedding band and here I was standing there wearing a $30.00 cluster.

After the wedding, my spirits were low because I knew I had married the wrong man. Everyone proceeded to the reception; I sat down and looked around the majority of the time and made myself smile. A lot of gifts and money were given. The only time I got up is when I slow danced with Jim on a couple of songs. My maid of honor and best friend at the time asked me was I okay? I told her no. But before I could tell her how I felt, someone came and pulled her on the dance floor. I got up and went outside for some fresh air and to pinch myself to see if I really went through with the wedding.

Oh yeah, everything was true and I began to cry again. My Dad came outside and once again I put on a fake smile. He was getting ready to go home and just wanted to say Congratulations. I hugged him and he left, taking my son with him, and I remained outside looking at the rainfall down upon the cars.

Around 2:00 a.m., I was still standing outside and from nowhere a little old lady came up to me and said, "Wow, I like your dress." I said thank you. She said, "You don't look happy and you also look as if you've been crying." I told her I just made one of the biggest mistakes in my life.

She replied by saying, I know. I asked her how did she know. She said she could feel my sadness. She also told me that she didn't mean to make this worse but she had to let me know that my troubles were just starting. When I asked her how? She looked up at the sky and said, Honey you are going to cry many tears." As she began to walk away, it seemed as if she just vanished. I got scared so I went back on the inside to join the wedding party and the other guests. I never told anybody about the little old lady. But, boy was she right.

The next day after everything was over, there was no honeymoon, no good morning, and no I love you or anything that newlyweds would do. Jim went to some of his friends' house and I talked on the telephone with my Mom and pretended as if I was happy. I couldn't find the words to tell my Mom she was right about everything. I lied and told her Jim was working and that everything couldn't be better. After the conversation ended with my Mom, my sister and I spoke briefly. She asked me was I happy and once again I lied because I didn't want to say anything to reveal the truth and have her go back and tell my Mom they were right.

Jim came home later on that afternoon. I didn't say too much to him. He asked where was the wedding ring? I told him it was upstairs in the drawer. He asked why I didn't have it on? I told him because that was not a wedding ring, that it was what most would call a friendship ring. I guess I gave him a reason to hang out all night long. Jim hung out so much after we got married until it didn't bother me.

Around 1993 we separated for a while. I would take my son over Jim' s Mom's house so he could baby-sit while I worked. School was out for the summer. Every afternoon when I would pick my son up from Jim 's Mom's house, he would say, "My Daddy's girlfriend came over and they sat real close together." I didn't pay it any attention for a while until he started saying the young lady's name. I tried to sneak up on them a couple of times by leaving work early to see who this young lady was. Jim and I were still married but I told him it was best if he left for a while so I could get my thoughts together.

I never caught Jim when I was trying to,but he did slip and once again I remained in an unhealthy relationship because I thought I had to be there. About a month or two later, Jim came back home - still not working a full time job. He would work jobs where he would get paid under the table like detailing cars because he was wanted for child support for a previous child. After about six months Jim found him a full-time job and stated he was ready to start acting like a father and a husband. He did well for a while.

In March, 1994, I started getting really sick. I had no idea what was wrong. I went to the doctor. They gave me some news that I didn't accept in the beginning. They told me I was two months pregnant. The first question that came to my mind was, how? The nurse laughed and said, "You know how." I told her that I had an eight-year-old son and hadn't used birth control for years. She told me, "Well it's time for another one."

Once again, I cried. Not because I was pregnant, but because I knew one day it would be just me and two kids. When I was five months pregnant, I told Jim I was pregnant and he immediately quit his job. He felt as if he needed to be home with me because I had become very ill and the doctor took me out of work.

I went back to the doctor and told him that I had to work because I had no income but a gang of bills. He agreed for me to work, but not all day and they would assign me to have a home nurse to visit twice a week. My income decreased tremendously. I found myself at the Social Services office applying for food stamps just to keep my son fed. Before the baby was born, I was given W.I.C. (Women Infant & Children Assistance) so I could stay healthy.

During the eighth month of my pregnancy, I got really sick at work and went home early. Jim was there but when I opened the door to go in the house, I saw three people running out the front door. I walked very fast to try and get a glimpse but I didn't recognize any of them. As I began to walk around the house, I smelled something burning. When I turned to look at the stove, to my surprise, I saw that Jim and his friends were cooking up some crack rocks. I started to call the police but once again I felt sympathetic and felt like I needed Jim to be there when the baby was born.

Jim was gone for approximately four hours. I cleaned my house, got my son off the school bus, cooked and prepared myself for the next work day. Later on that night, when Jim came home, he was apologetic. He said he was doing that so he could get money to help out with the bills. We got in a fight and yes, I was still pregnant.

It's October, my ninth month and now I'm at home for good. Things between Jim and I had not improved. I was big as a house and ready to have the baby. On October 12th, Jim went with me to the doctor for the first time. The doctor began running tests and asking me was I okay. I told her, yes. She asked me to have a seat in the waiting room until my results came back. Jim and I waited for approximately two hours. We weren't talking, just sitting there looking at all those pregnant women -- some eating, some hurting, some just finding out they were pregnant.

I saw a nurse coming towards me with a wheelchair. She asked me was my name Derbin and I said yes. She said, " I want you to come with me." I asked, "For what?" She said, Because if you don't come with me, you might die if you go home. I told her I guess I'm going to have to die because I'm not ready to have this baby today. I resisted for about 20 minutes. I told her I needed to go home to get my suitcase and to make sure my bills were caught up. I came up with so many excuses until I just got tired of lying. I finally sat in the wheelchair and was taken to Labor and Delivery.

Jim followed and promised to take care of everything. I got more worried - not about my bills - but about my eight year old son. On the fourth day at the hospital, my labor was induced because my blood pressure was so high. My daughter came into this world on October 16, 1994. I don't remember delivering her because I had a C-section. I do remember when I came to, I was hurting really bad.

Two days had gone. The nurses would come in to see how I was doing. I didn't really see the baby because I was so drugged up. One of the nurses told me that it had been three days and I still haven't seen my daughter. I told her I didn't want to see her because I was hurting and I was tired. She said it was the anesthesia and that the doctor was concerned.

They thought I was having a bout with depression. I was very sad but didn't want anyone to know. On my fourth day in the hospital, I decided to try to walk to see my daughter. It took me 30 minutes to get to the baby room. I had 15 staples in my stomach. It was a short walk to the baby room, but a long walk for me because I had trouble walking.

As I pushed the baby to my room, I looked at her and all I could see was me. My daughter looks just like me. She is my twin. After I got situated and held my daughter for the first time, Jim came to visit along with my son. While I was holding the baby, my son climbed in the bed with us. I told Jim he could leave and to pick my son up later on that night. I had been gone away from home for eight days.

When Jim left my son began to cry as he lay beside me. I asked him what was wrong and he said, "I can't tell you or I'll get in trouble." I looked at him and asked him to bring the baby's bed over so I can put her in it. When he did, I turned over and looked at his wet face and asked him again what was wrong? He made me promise not to tell. I promised. He said that he hadn't eaten nor had he watched television. When he got off the bus he would be home by himself for a while. He said he had to get his own clothes together and half of them were dirty because Jim hadn't washed clothes. I asked him what happened to the television. He said Jim let the next door neighbor use it because we had three. He gave away the largest one. After I received that news, I buzzed the nurse and told her that I was going home that night.

I pulled the I.V. out of my hand, put my clothes on and was ready to check out. It took three doctors to tell me I wasn't going anywhere. I told them they didn't understand. I had to go because my son's life was in jeopardy. The doctors met for about an hour and agreed to release me but not that day, the next day.

I asked if it was okay if my son could stay the night with me at the hospital. They agreed. As the night went on my son was by my side sleeping peacefully. The nurses were in and out making sure my daughter had all her shots before her departure the next day. That night I didn't sleep at all. I sat up waiting for the sun to come up because I knew I was going home.

The next morning when my son woke up, he asked where was Jim. I told him I didn't know, but we'll get home one way or the other. When I called my house, Jim answered the telephone. I was pleasant. I told him I was coming home and needed him to pick me up now. He came to the hospital but was very puzzled about how early I was leaving. I was released along with a written prescription for an antibiotic which I agreed to take until the bottle was empty.

When we arrived home, I looked around the house and noticed a lot of my hard earned household supplies were missing. I confronted Jim and he said someone must have broken in the house. That was it! It was time for him to go. I didn't love him and he was just there giving me a headache and making me sicker. After I asked Jim to leave, he got really mad and began to tell me that no one will ever want me with two children. He told me I was too picky and too head strong. No man will want me. I told him that was fine. "I'll be by myself. At least I will have peace of mind." After about three months, I was doing fine enjoying life, inviting friends over, sitting down just talking and having a good time.

I eventually returned to work but shortly after resigning after seven years of employment with the company. I found a better paying job in the payroll department, making lots more money, getting paid every two weeks instead of once a month.

Just The Other Woman

Jim would call to see if he could visit the children and sometimes I would let him. After my separation became final, Jim started getting into trouble. Late one night, his mom called and told me that Jim was in jail for stealing. Prior to that, he stayed in trouble with the police because of a drug habit and child support. I told his mom that wasn't my problem any more. I was done with Jim . Jim was in jail for a year for a number of charges against him.

After Jim got out of jail, he decided to come by my house unannounced. I told him if he didn't leave I would call the police. I had a male friend at that time. I met him on the new job. Jim would call the job and harass Colin and me. Jim called the president of the company and told lies about me and Colin . Colin and I had to meet with the president. Neither one of us was fired. Jim sure did try to get us fired. Jim was very upset because I finally moved on. Years ago he had made a comment that I would never leave him because I didn't have the guts to be by myself.

In 1998, I became very close to Colin. I thought this was the man whom I was meant to be with in the beginning. Colin was a strong man.

He moved me from the old place to a new place and dared Jim to come where he was paying rent. Jim stayed away and eventually came to terms that what we had was over and it was time to let go.

I ran into Jim and he apologized for taking advantage of our relationship, and he missed me and wished I could give him another chance. I finally had the courage to tell him no and that our marriage was one big joke. I knew there were other women involved but I had gotten to the point where I didn't care. There was nothing he could say or do to get me back. I tried to be his friend for the sake of the children, but that didn't work either. Whenever I asked for money to help with the children, he told me I needed to ask my boyfriend. I let him know that the children were not the boyfriend's responsibility; they were his. He still refused to help.

Colin took the role as father. He didn't have children, but he knew exactly what to do. Colin paid bills, bought Christmas, bought school clothes, bought groceries. We didn't live together but oftentimes when I came in from work, I knew he was there because he would always leave a token of his love behind. Throughout the relationship, I would receive expensive gifts but never questioned where the money came from. I knew Colin had a job but the job wasn't rewarding enough to afford the luxuries that were lavished upon me.

After becoming quite comfortable in our relationship, I asked Colin about the extra money and he told me that he had a small business of his own and I asked what was the name of his company and he told me that he sold drugs on the side. I never dated a drug dealer. I was on the other end of being with a drug user. Colin and I agreed that he would not bring drugs in my home or around my children. He didn't

I felt bad because people would buy the drugs and I knew that a household was being torn apart behind those drugs. My powerlessness had me believing that since I didn't have to see these people, I only saw the end result which, was the cash. Colin made so much money that he bought everything cash. He even bought thousands of dollars of furniture in cash. I thought this was the lifestyle that I could get used to. There was nothing I didn't ask for from Colin and I didn't get.

Colin was a nice young man and came from a Christian background, but he got involved with the wrong crowd. He often went out house hunting. He always wanted me to live in a house and said he would pay for everything. We never got to move into the house because after a year into the relationship, I began to see traits in Colin that I saw in Jim. Colin started telling lies of his whereabouts and began to think that money could keep me quiet. Colin wined and dined me with nice things, but it was something else there that I needed to know. When I began asking Colin questions, he started getting close enough to me so that I wouldn't be so suspicious. I came home from work one day and Colin had moved some of his belongings into my house. I didn't mind him moving in because I felt like I could keep a close eye on him.

Our relationship grew very strong. We went to Florida to visit my Mom and sister. They liked him but Mom said, "Don't ever put all your trust in a man." I listened and that was all I did. When we returned home,

Colin said he was going to his brother's house to check in and let them know he made it back. He was gone approximately three hours.

When he came home I was in the bed and so were the children. Around 1:00 a.m., Colin got in bed and fell off to sleep. At 3:00 a.m. a noise woke me up. I didn't wake anyone up at first. I tipped into the living room and heard a rattling noise. I thought, "Oh my God, somebody is trying to break in the house." I was scared. I went into the kitchen, open the drawer and pulled out a long knife. I walked to the front door and looked out the peep hole and saw nothing. Once again, I heard the rattling noise. I walked over to the living room, looked down on the rug and there I saw Colin's pager hitting against my lead table. I picked up the pager and began to press buttons. Colin had an alpha pager so I could read his messages. As I began to read the messages, my eyes got big. A young woman wrote, "Where are you? You need to get in touch with me ASAP. I know you're back from Florida with your boys. You could have called to say everything was okay." I was shocked all over again. I knew our relationship was too good to be true.

I didn't confront Colin right away. Oh boy, what had I come across! Sometimes it's not good to snoop because you will end up getting your feelings hurt. I snooped about a month. I would hit redial when Colin used my telephone. That redial button would make you regret being nosey. Thanks to redial, I ended up with Colin's pass code to his voice mail. I called that voice mail every day and almost every hour because I knew a message was there.

The woman on the voice mail was a person who had been hurting for five years. Every year Colin was with a different woman the entire time they were dating. I heard tears of hurt, tears of anger and years of wasted time. I decided to come clean with Colin about everything, and of course he denied being in a relationship with this woman. Since I was the bigger person, I decided to give this young lady a call and get her side of the story. To my surprise, Colin was just with her a couple of days ago. She said Colin was with her when Hurricane Floyd hit. We continued to talk and she asked me could I meet her? When we met, she had on an engagement ring. She had pictures and a lot of other evidence to show that they were still together. The entire time she talked and pulled things out of her purse. I was crying on the inside because once again, I chose the wrong man.

All kinds of thoughts started going through my mind, including killing Colin. She got on her cellular phone and asked Colin if he would meet her so they could go out for dinner. Colin agreed, so she told him where she was. He had no idea I was standing beside her. We waited for his arrival patiently and anxiously to hear the excuses on how we know each other. He never showed up so we went to him. He said he knew something was wrong. That's why he didn't come. After everything was exposed, Colin said he tried to love two women. I got tired of all the back and forth about why this and why that. I decided to leave.

My ride home was long. Not only was I involved in this chaos, but so were my two children. It took me a while to tell my children that Colin will not be coming around any more. When I told them, sadness came upon their faces because we believed Colin was "the one." I was dating Colin but he wasn't dating me.

Two weeks passed, and I was a total wreck. I went into a depression and could think about nothing but payback. I told a lot of people about my incident and was hoping that someone would hurt Colin as bad as he hurt me. Instead the young lady was targeted. One of my friends overheard me talking about where Colin's girlfriend was employed. Colin's girlfriend and I did the same job, but worked at different companies. She was called and harassed on her job by a few of my associates. I didn't know they were calling her as often as they were until one fateful morning in February, the police came knocking on my door to deliver a summons to appear in court. After looking over the summons to appear in court, the date for me to be in court had passed. I asked the police, What do I do now?" He said, "Have the case re-opened, or it will stay on your record." I wasn't targeting her, I was targeting Colin. I guess she got upset because I made it hard for Colin. After three years, I had the case re-opened so this foolishness wouldn't be held against me. I was a bail bondsman at the time so I knew a lot of people. I hired an attorney to represent me because it was my word against hers. After the evidence was presented and heard, it was dismissed because years had passed and it was foolish. God was in the midst.

Accepting Christ

I started living my life as a true Christian. Times were hard and so were the struggles. I was evicted from my apartment in 2000. I turned to my biological father for help but his wife didn't want us around. She made it plain and simple. His children were not allowed to stay in their home. With no place to turn, my father's first cousin took in my children and me. We stayed with her until the end of December 2000. Since I was a bail bondsman, I made money daily. I decided to get a hotel room for one night. One night turned into four months. That hotel became our home. I was devastated. I began to think, "What if I go back in the world and do worldly things; I wouldn't be in this mess." All sorts of negativity came to mind, even prostitution. No, thank God, I never became a prostitute. I was stronger than that.

On April 13, 2001, in the hotel, I fell on my knees to pray while my children were asleep. I asked God to please help me find somewhere for my children to live. I felt I had failed as a mother. One minute we had lots and the next we had nothing but clothes. God answers prayers.

My son played AAU basketball, and his coach called my cellular phone to see if my son was going to play in the game that weekend. My cellular phone went dead as soon as I was getting ready to call the coach back. I hesitated for a few minutes, found a phone, called him back. He asked, "What are you doing at a hotel?" God wouldn't let me lie so I began to cry. He asked, "Which location are you at?" When I told him, he told me to start packing my things because that was my last day there. When Coach arrived, he was teary eyed. He asked why didn't I tell him? I said I didn't want anybody in my business. He said, A hungry mouth won't get fed if it's closed." He began to tell me that on the AAU team, there is a parent who rents apartments. I simply did not know because I did not ask. You have not, because you ask not.

After the lecture was given, I followed him to the complex where the parent worked as well as owned these apartments. Coach explained my situation. She took us on the inside and I filled out the paper work without giving her one brown penny. Oh, look at God. Hallelujah! I stayed in her complex one year then I moved on. God has really been providing.

Since I found a permanent job, I have paid my tithes on a regular basis. I have joined a wonderful church where the Pastor teaches as he preaches. My faith in God has gotten strong. There is nothing too hard for God. God puts us in situations because when we come out, he wants us to spread His goodness and give Him all the glory and praise.

Conclusion

I hope these words will inspire and empower women and let them know that being in a bad relationship is not healthy. You don't have to be there. There is a way out. It took me twelve years to get out of one bad situation and one and a half years to get out of another bad situation. I have endured a lot of hurt and a lot of pain. Thanks be to God and his mercy, He brought me out of both situations.

I know, we, women don't like being alone, but sometimes alone is best from someone who treats you wrong. My relationship with God has become very strong and as long as I continue to seek Him and trust Him, He'll one day send His best.

No matter who may hurt you and no matter how bad they hurt you, you always have to have room in your heart for forgiveness. It is only then that the Lord can use you.

Proverbs 23:13-12 - Withhold not correction from the child: for if thou beatest him with the rod, he shall not die. Thou shalt beat him with the rod, and shalt deliver his soul from hell.

Psalms 32:8 - I will instruct thee and teach thee in the way which thou shalt go; I will guide thee with mine eye.

Psalms 37:40 - And the Lord shall help them and deliver them: He shall deliver them from the wicked, and save them because they trust Him.

Psalms 37:4 Delight thyself also in the Lord and he shall give thee the Desires of thine heart.

Psalms(55:17-18) Evening and morning and at noon,will I pray and cry aloud: And he shall hear my voice. He hath delivered my soul in peace from the battle that was against me: For there were many with me.

Proverbs (3:5-12) Trust in the Lord with all thine heart; and lean not

Unto thine own understanding.

In all thy ways acknowledge him,and he shall direct thy paths.

Be not wise in thine own eyes: fear the Lord,and depart from evil.

It shall be health to thy navel and marrow to thy bones.

Honour the Lord with thy substance,and with the firstfruits of

All thine increase.

So shall thy barns be filled with plenty,and thy presses shall burst out with new wine.

My son despise not the chastening of the Lord: neither be weary of his correction.

For whom the Lord loveth he correcteth: even as a father the son in whom he delighteth.

Proverbs(13:11) Wealth gotten by vanity shall be diminished: but he that Gathereth by labour shall increase.

Proverbs (23:17) Let not thine heart envy sinners; but be thou in the fear of the Lord all the day long.

Proverbs (29:23) A man's pride shall bring him low: but honour shall uphold The humble spirit.

Matthew(6:9:15) Our father which art in heaven hallowed be thy name thy Kingdom come ,thy will be done in earth ,as it is in heaven give us this day

Our daily bread and forgive us our debts,as we forgive our debtors, and lead Us not into temptation, but deliver us from evil: for thine is the kingdom, and the the power and the glory forever Amen.

(14) For if ye forgive men their trespasses your heavenly father will also forgive you.

(15) But if ye forgive not men their trespasses, neither will your father forgive your trespasses.

Ecclesiastes (3:1) To everything there is a season,and a time to every purpose Under the heaven.

Matthew (4:4) But he answered and said it is written, Man shall not live by bread alone, but by every word that proceedeth out of the mouth of God.

Matthew (21:22) And all things, whatsoever ye shall ask in prayer, Believing ye shall receive.

About The Author

The author of Unnecessary Suffering was born tenacious. She was brought down by man for a short period of time, only to find out who she was and her purpose in life. She's a comforter when one is down, she's witty when one needs a laugh, she's bold when speaking about the Lord, she's sympathetic to others and will give you her last. When God made her, he made a woman with tact. Lord thank you for deliverance, thank you for closing doors of the past and opening doors to the future.